Words in the Mourning Time

Words
in the
Mourning
Time

Poems by Robert Hayden

October House Inc · New York

ACKNOWLEDGMENTS

Some of these poems were first published in *Anon*, the "To-day's Poets" section of the *Chicago Tribune Sunday Magazine*, *For Malcolm X*, *Thoroughbred*, *Generation*, and *World Order: A Baha'i Magazine*.

"And All the Atoms Cry Aloud" was written for the Baha'i Centennial celebration held in Chicago, October 1967.

"Locus," "On Lookout Mountain," "The Lions," "Lear is Gay," and Part One of "Aunt Jemima of the Ocean Waves" are revisions of poems from previous collections.

Published by October House Inc
55 West Thirteenth Street, New York, N.Y. 10011

Copyright © 1970 by Robert Hayden
All rights reserved

Library of Congress Catalogue Card Number 74–99499
ISBN Cloth 0–8079–0159–8
ISBN Paper 0–8079–0160–1

For Marie Alice Hanson
and Louis Martin
with gratitude

Contents

four

one:

SPHINX

If he could solve the riddle,
she would not leap
        from those gaunt rocks to her death,
but devour him instead.

It pleasures her to hold
him captive there—
        to keep him in the reach of her
blood-matted paws.

It is your fate, she has often
said, to endure
        my riddling. Your fate to live
at the mercy of my

conundrum, which, in truth,
is only a kind
        of psychic joke. No, you shall
not leave this place.

(Consider anyway the view from
here.) In time,
        you will come to regard my questioning
with a certain pained

amusement; in time, get so
you would hardly find
        it possible to live without
my joke and me.

THE DREAM

(1863)

That evening Sinda thought she heard the drums
and hobbled from her cabin to the yard.
    The quarters now were lonely-still in willow dusk
after the morning's ragged jubilo,
    when laughing crying singing the folks went off
with Marse Lincum's soldier boys.
    But Sinda hiding would not follow them: those
Buckras with their ornery
    funning, cussed commands, oh they were not were not
the hosts the dream had promised her.

    and hope when these few lines reaches your hand they
will fine you well. I am tired some but it is war you
know and ole jeff Davis muss be ketch an hung to a sour
apple tree like it says in the song I seen some akshun
but that is what i listed for not to see the sights ha ha
More of our peeples coming every day. the Kernul calls
them contrybans and has them work aroun the Camp
and learning to be soljurs. How is the wether home. Its
warm this evening but theres been lots of rain

    How many times that dream had come to her—
more vision than a dream—
    the great big soldiers marching out of gunburst,
their faces those of Cal and Joe
    and Charlie sold to the ricefields oh sold away
a-many and a-many a long year ago.
    Fevered, gasping, Sinda listened, knew this was
the ending of her dream and prayed
    that death, grown fretful and impatient, nagging her,
would wait a little longer, would let her see.

and we been marching sleeping too in cold rain and mirey mud a heap a times. Tell Mama Thanks for The Bible an not worry so. Did brother fix the roof yet like he promised? this mus of been a real nice place befor the fighting uglied it all up the judas trees is blosommed out so pretty same as if this hurt and truble wasnt going on. Almos like somthing you mite dream about i take it for a sign The Lord remembers Us Theres talk we will be moving into Battle very soon agin

Trembling tottering Hep me Jesus Sinda crossed
the wavering yard, reached
        a redbud tree in bloom, could go no farther, clung
to the bole and clinging fell
        to her knees. She tried to stand, could not so much
as lift her head, tried to hold
        the bannering sounds, heard only the whipoorwills
in tenuous moonlight; struggled to rise
        and make her way to the road to welcome Joe and Cal
and Charlie, fought with brittle strength to rise.

So pray for me that if the Bullit with my name rote on it get me it will not get me in retreet i do not think them kine of thots so much no need in Dying till you die I all ways figger, course if the hardtack and the bullybeef do not kill me nuthing can i guess. Tell Joe I hav shure seen me some ficety gals down here in Dixieland & i mite jus go ahead an jump over the broomstick with one and bring her home, well I muss close with Love to all & hope to see you soon Yrs Cal

" 'MYSTERY BOY' LOOKS FOR KIN IN NASHVILLE"

Puzzle faces in the dying elms
promise him treats if he will stay.
Sometimes they hiss and spit at him
like varmints caught
in a thicket of butterflies.

A black doll,
one disremembered time,
came floating down to him
through mimosa's fancywork leaves and blooms
to be his hidden bride.

From the road beyond the creepered walls
they call to him now and then,
and he'll take off in spite of the angry trees,
hearing like the loudening of his heart
the name he never can he never can repeat.

And when he gets to where the voices were—
Don't cry, his dollbaby wife implores;
I know where they are, don't cry.
We'll go and find them, we'll go
and ask them for your name again.

THE BROKEN DARK

Sleepless, I stare
from the dark hospital room
at shadows of a flower and its leaves
the nightlight fixes like a blotto
on the corridor wall. Shadow-plays
of Bali—demons move to the left,
gods, in their frangipani crowns
and gold, to the right.
Ah and my life
in the shadow of God's laser light—
shadow of deformed homunculus?
A fool's errand given by fools.
Son, go fetch a pint of pigeon's milk
from the drugstore and be quick.
Demons on the left. Death on either side,
the Rabbi said, the way of life between.
That groaning. Man with his belly slashed,
two-timing lover. Dying?
The nightnurse rustles by.
Struggles in the pit. I have come back
to tell thee of struggles in the pit.
Perhaps is dying.
Free of pain, my own death still
a theorem to be proved.
Alláh'u'Abbhá. O Healing Spirit,
Thy nearness our forgiving cure.

THE MIRAGES

Exhaustion among rocks
    in rockfall sun;

    thirst, and thick
water to drink,

    the stranger said.

And the mirages, the
    mirages —

    I knew what they were
yet often

changed my course
    and followed them.

    Less lonely, less
lonely then,

    the stranger said.

SOLEDAD

(And I, I am no longer of that world)

Naked, he lies in the blinded room
chainsmoking, cradled by drugs, by jazz
as never by any lover's cradling flesh.

Miles Davis coolly blows for him:
O pena negra, sensual Flamenco blues;
the red clay foxfire voice of Lady Day

(lady of the pure black magnolias)
sobsings her sorrow and loss and fare you well,
dryweeps the pain his treacherous jailers

have released him from for awhile.
His fears and his unfinished self
await him down in the anywhere streets.

He hides on the dark side of the moon,
takes refuge in a stained-glass cell,
flies to a clockless country of crystal.

Only the ghost of Lady Day knows where
he is. Only the music. And he swings
oh swings: beyond complete immortal now.

AUNT JEMIMA OF THE OCEAN WAVES

I

Enacting someone's notion of themselves
(and me), The One And Only Aunt Jemima
and Kokimo The Dixie Dancing Fool
do a bally for the freak show.

I watch a moment, then move on,
pondering the logic that makes of them
(and me) confederates
of The Spider Girl, The Snake-skinned Man. . .

Poor devils have to live somehow.

I cross the boardwalk to the beach,
lie in the sand and gaze beyond
the clutter at the sea.

II
Trouble you for a light?
I turn as Aunt Jemima settles down
beside me, her blue-rinsed hair
without the red bandanna now.

I hold the lighter to her cigarette.
Much obliged. Unmindful (perhaps)
of my embarrassment, she looks
at me and smiles: You sure

do favor a friend I used to have.
Guess that's why I bothered you
for a light. So much like him that I—
She pauses, watching white horses rush

to the shore. Way them big old waves
come slamming whopping in,
sometimes it's like they mean to smash
this no-good world to hell.

   Well, it could happen. A book I read—
Crossed that very ocean years ago.
London, Paris, Rome,
Constantinople too—I've seen them all.

Back when they billed me everywhere
as the Sepia High Stepper.
Crowned heads applauded me.
Years before your time. Years and years.

I wore me plenty diamonds then,
and counts or dukes or whatever they were
would fill my dressing room
with the costliest flowers. But of course

there was this one you resemble so.
Get me? The sweetest gentleman.
Dead before his time. Killed in the war
to save the world for another war.

High-stepping days for me
were over after that. Still I'm not one
to let grief idle me for long.
I went out with a mental act—

mind-reading—Mysteria From
The Mystic East—veils and beads
and telling suckers how to get
stolen rings and sweethearts back.

One night he was standing by my bed,
seen him plain as I see you,
and warned me without a single word:
Baby, quit playing with spiritual stuff.

So here I am, so here I am,
fake mammy to God's mistakes.
And that's the beauty part,
I mean, ain't that the beauty part.

She laughs, but I do not, knowing what
her laughter shields. And mocks.
I light another cigarette for her.
She smokes, not saying any more.

Scream of children in the surf,
adagios of sun and flashing foam,
the sexual glitter, oppressive fun. . . .
An antique etching comes to mind:

"The Sable Venus" naked on
a baroque Cellini shell—voluptuous
imago floating in the wake
of slave-ships on fantastic seas.

Jemima sighs, Reckon I'd best
be getting back. I help her up.
Don't you take no wooden nickels, hear?
Tin dimes neither. So long, pal.

two:

LOCUS

(for Ralph)

Here redbuds like momentary trees
    of an illusionist;
here Cherokee rose, acacia, and mimosa;
here magnolias—totemic flowers
    wreathing legends of this place.
Here violent metamorphosis,
    with every blossom turning
deadly and memorial soldiers,
their sabres drawn, charging
    firewood shacks,
apartheid streets. Here wound-red earth
    and blinding cottonfields,
rock hills where sachems counseled,
where scouts gazed stealthily
    upon the glittering death march
of De Soto through Indian wilderness.
    Here mockingbird and
cottonmouth, fury of rivers.
Here swamp and trace and bayou
    where the runagate hid,
the devil with Spanish pistols rode.
    Here spareness, rankness, harsh
brilliances; beauty of what's hardbitten,
knotted, stinted, flourishing
    in despite, on thorny meagerness
thriving, twisting into grace.
    Here symbol houses
where the brutal dream lives out its lengthy
dying. Here the past, adored and
    unforgiven. Here the past—
soulscape, Old Testament battleground
of warring shades whose weapons kill.

ON LOOKOUT MOUNTAIN

I listen for the sounds of cannon, cries
vibrating still upon the air,
timeless echoes in echoic time—
imagine how they circle out and out

concentric with Kilroy's cries,
as beyond the tangent calm
of this midcentury morning he burns
or freezes in the warfare of our peace.

I gaze through layered light,
think of the death-for-foothold inching climb
of Union soldiers struggling up
the crackling mountainside.

And here where Sunday alpinists
pick views and souvenirs,
here daring choices stained
the clouds with dubious victory.

A world away, yet nearer than our hope
or our belief, the scions of that fighting climb
endless hills of war, amid war's peaks
and valleys broken, scattered fall.

Have done, have done. Behold how bright
upon the mountain the gadget feet
of trivia shine.
Oh, hear the stuffed gold eagle sing.

KODACHROMES OF THE ISLAND

I

Halfnaked children
met us singing for coins
at the swaybacked jetty.

Gold brooms had swept
the mist away, and
the island air was clear.

Parrot and zinnia
colors teemed
in thronging sunlight.

A young beggar greeted us
Dios se lo pague
with fingerless hands.

II
Out on the yellow
as pollen or sulphur
lake Indian fishermen,

naked torsos oiled with
sunlight, were casting
their mariposas.

On the landing, women
were cleaning a catch and
tossing the guts to

squealing piglets. A tawny
butterfly drunkenly circled
then lighted on offal.

III

Black turkeys children
dogs foraged and played
under drying fishnets.

Vendors urged laquerwork
and glazed angels
with candles between their wings.

Alien, at home—as always
everywhere—I roamed
the cobbled island,

and thought of Yeats,
his passionate search for
a theme. Sought mine.

ZEUS OVER REDEYE

(The Redstone Arsenal)

Enclave where new mythologies
of power come to birth—
where coralled energy and power breed
like prized man-eating animals.
Like dragon, hydra, basilisk.

Radar corollas and Holland tulips
the colors of Easter eggs
form vistas for the ironist.
Where elm, ailanthus, redbud grew
parabola and gantry rise.

In soaring stasis rocket missiles loom,
the cherished weapons named for Nike
(O headless armless Victory),
for Zeus, Apollo, Hercules—
eponyms of redeyed fury
greater, lesser than their own.

Ignorant outlander, mere civilian,
not sure always of what it is
I see, I walk with you among
these totems of our fire-breathing age,
question and question you,

who are at home in terra guarded like
a sacred phallic grove.
Your partial answers reassure
me less than they appall.
I feel as though invisible fuses were

burning all around us burning all
around us. Heat-quiverings twitch
danger's hypersensitive skin.
The very sunlight here seems flammable.
And shadows give
us no relieving shade.

UNIDENTIFIED FLYING OBJECT

It's true Mattie Lee
has clean disappeared.
And shouldn't we notify
the sheriff? No use, Will
insists, no earthly use.

He was sleeping one off
under the trees that night,
he claims, and woke up when
the space-ship
landed—a silvery dome

with gassy-green and red-
hot-looking lights like eyes
that stared blinked stared.
Says he hid himself
in the bushes and watched,

shaking. Pretty soon
a hatch slides open, a ramp
glides forward like
a glowing tongue poked out.
And who or what is it

silently present there?
Same as if Will's
trying to peer through webs
and bars of gauzy glare
screening, distorting a shape

he sees yet cannot see.
But crazier than that
was when Mattie Lee
came running from her house
towards the thing.

She's wearing her sunflower hat
and the dress the lady she cooked
for gave her, and it's like
she's late for work the way
she scurries up the ramp.

And it seems to Will
that in its queer
shining, plain Mattie Lee's
transformed—is every teasing brown
he's ever wanted, never had.

He's fixing to shout, Come back,
Mattie Lee, come back;
but a heavy hand is over his mouth
when he hears her laugh
as she steps inside

without even a goodbye glance
around. The next Will knew,
the UFO rose in the air—
no blastoff roar, no flame,
he says—hung in the dark,

hovered, shimmered,
its eyes pulsing, then whirred
spiraling into the sky,
vanished as though
it had never been.

Will's tale anyhow.
All I'm certain of
is Mattie Lee's
nowhere to be found
and must have gone

off in a hurry. Left her doors
unlocked and the radio on
and a roast in the oven. Strange.
As for Will, he's a changed man,
not drinking nowadays and sad.

Mattie Lee's friends—
she's got no kinfolks, lived
alone—are worried, swear
Will was craving her
and she held herself too good

for him, being head of Mount
Nebo's usher board and such.
And some are hinting what I,
for one—well, never mind.
The talk is getting mean.

three:

words in the mourning time

(for David Way)

EL-HAJJ MALIK EL-SHABAZZ

(Malcolm X)
O masks and metamorphoses of Ahab, Native Son

I

The icy evil that struck his father down
and ravished his mother into madness
trapped him in violence of a punished self
struggling to break free.

As Home Boy, as Dee-troit Red,
he fled his name, became the quarry of
his own obsessed pursuit.

He conked his hair and Lindy-hopped,
zoot-suited jiver, swinging those chicks
in the hot rose and reefer glow.

His injured childhood bullied him.
He skirmished in the Upas trees
and cannibal flowers of the American Dream—

but could not hurt the enemy
powered against him there.

II

Sometimes the dark that gave his life
its cold satanic sheen would shift
a little, and he saw himself
floodlit and eloquent;

yet how could he, "Satan" in The Hole,
guess what the waking dream foretold?

Then false dawn of vision came;
he fell upon his face before
a racist Allah pledged to wrest him from
the hellward-thrusting hands of Calvin's Christ—

to free him and his kind
from Yakub's white-faced treachery.
He rose redeemed from all but prideful anger,

though adulterate attars could not cleanse
him of the odors of the pit.

III
Asalam alaikum!

He X'd his name, became his people's anger,
exhorted them to vengeance for their past;
rebuked, admonished them,

their scourger who
would shame them, drive them from
the lush ice gardens of their servitude.

Asalam alaikum!

Rejecting Ahab, he was of Ahab's tribe.
"Strike through the mask!"

IV

Time. "The martyr's time," he said.
Time and the karate killer,
knifer, gunman. Time that brought
ironic trophies as his faith

twined sparking round the bole,
the fruit of neo-Islam.
"The martyr's time."

But first, the ebb time pilgrimage
toward revelation, hejira to
his final metamorphosis;

Labbayk! Labbayk!

He fell upon his face before
Allah the raceless in whose blazing Oneness all
were one. He rose renewed renamed, became
much more than there was time for him to be.

WORDS IN THE MOURNING TIME

I

For King, for Robert Kennedy,
destroyed by those they could not save,
for King for Kennedy I mourn.
And for America, self-destructive, self-betrayed.

I grieve. Yet know the vanity
of grief—through power of
The Blessed Exile's
transilluminating word

aware of how these deaths, how all
the agonies of our deathbed childbed age
are process, major means whereby,
oh dreadfully, our humanness must be achieved.

II
Killing people to save, to free them?
With napalm lighting routes to the future?

III

He comes to my table in his hungry wounds
and his hunger. The flamed-out eyes,
their sockets dripping. The nightmare mouth.

He snatches food from my plate, raw
fingers bleeding, seizes my glass
and drinks, leaving flesh-fragments on its rim.

IV

Vietnam bloodclotted name in my consciousness
recurring and recurring
like the obsessive thought many midnights
now of my own dying

Vietnam and I think of the villages
mistakenly burning the schoolrooms devouring
their children and I think of those who
were my students
                    brutalized killing
wasted by horror
in ultimate loneliness
dying
              Vietnam Vietnam

V

Oh, what a world we make,
oppressor and oppressed.

Our world—
this violent ghetto, slum
of the spirit raging against itself.

We hate kill destroy
in the name of human good
our killing and our hate destroy.

VI

Lord Riot

      naked

           in flaming clothes

cannibal ruler

         of anger's

             carousals

   sing hey nonny no

terror

    his tribute

          shriek of bloody glass

his praise

   sing wrathful sing vengeful

     sing hey nonny no

gigantic

    and laughing

          sniper on tower

I hate

    I destroy

      I am   I am

    sing hey nonny no

    sing burn baby burn

VII

voice in the wilderness

Know that love has chosen you
to live his crucial purposes.
Know that love has chosen you.

And will not pamper you nor spare;
demands obedience to all
the rigorous laws of risk,
does not pamper, will not spare.

Oh, master now love's instruments—
complex and not for the fearful,
simple and not for the foolish.
Master now love's instruments.

I who love you tell you this,
even as the pitiful killer waits for me,
I who love you tell you this.

VIII

Light and the
                distortions
                                of light as
the flame-night
                dawns
                                Zenith-time and the anger
unto death and the
                fire-focused
                                image
of a man
            invisible man
                            and black boy and native
son and the
            man who
                        lives underground whose
name nobody
                knows
                            harrowing havocking
running through
                holocaust
                            seeking the
soul-country of his
                meaning

48

IX

As the gook woman howls
for her boy in the smouldering,
as the expendable Clean-Cut Boys
From Decent American Homes
are slashing off enemy ears for keepsakes;

as the victories are tallied up
with flag-draped coffins, plastic bodybags,
what can I say
but this, this:

We must not be frightened nor cajoled
into accepting evil as deliverance from evil.
We must go on struggling to be human,
though monsters of abstraction
police and threaten us.

Reclaim now, now renew the vision of
a human world where godliness
is possible and man
is neither gook nigger honkey wop nor kike

but man

permitted to be man.

X

and all the atoms cry aloud

I bear Him witness now
Who by the light of suns beyond the suns beyond
   the sun with shrill pen

   revealed renewal of
the covenant of timelessness with time, proclaimed
   advent of splendor joy

   alone can comprehend
and the imperious evils of an age could not
   withstand and stars

   and stones and seas
acclaimed—His life its crystal image and
   magnetic field.

   I bear Him witness now—
mystery Whose major clues are the heart of man,
   the mystery of God:

   Bahá'u'lláh:
Logos, poet, cosmic hero, surgeon, architect
   of our hope of peace,

   wronged, exiled One,
chosen to endure what agonies of knowledge, what
   auroral dark

       bestowals of truth
vision power anguish for our future's sake.
       "I was but a man

       "like others, asleep upon
My couch, when, lo, the breezes of the All-Glorious
       were wafted over Me. . . ."

       Called, as in dead of night
a dreamer is roused to help the helpless flee
       a burning house.

       I bear Him witness now:
towards Him our history in its disastrous quest
       for meaning is impelled.

four:

MONET'S "WATERLILIES"

(for Bill and Sonja)

Today as the news from Selma and Saigon
poisons the air like fallout,
    I come again to see
the serene great picture that I love
and flames disfigured once
        and efficient evil may yet destroy.

Here space and time exist in light
the eye like the eye of faith believes.
    The seen, the known
dissolve in irridescence, become
illusive flesh of light
        that was not, was, forever is.

O light beheld as through refracting tears.
Here is the aura of that world
        each of us has lost.
Here is the shadow of its joy.

THE LIONS

With what panache, he said,
I bow to the applause,
    I open danger's door
while brasses hold their Ahs
    and set the mood
for courage leonine.
    And in the kingdom-cage
as I make my lions leap,
    through nimbus-fire leap,
oh, as I see them leap—
    unsparing beauty that
creates and serves my will,
    the savage real that clues
my vision of the real—
    my soul exults and Holy cries
and Holy Holy cries, he said.

OCTOBER

I
October—
its plangency, its glow

as of words in
the poet's mind,

as of God in
the saint's.

II

I wept for your mother
in her pain, wept in
my joy when you were
born,
          Maia,
that October morning.
We named you
for a star a star-like
poem sang.
               I write this
for your birthday
and say I love you
and say October
like the phoenix sings you.

III

This chiming
and tolling
    of lion
and phoenix
and chimera
    colors.
This huntsman's
horn, sounding
    mort for
quarry fleeing
through mirrors
    of burning
into deathless
    dying.

IV
Rockweight
of surprising snow

crushed
the October trees,

broke
branches that

crashing set
the snow on fire.

THE RETURN

(after Pasternak)

Rooms are grotesque with furniture of snow,
ice blisters the hair of portraits;
spiderwebs of snow and ice
are skeleton stars in wolf-wind gloom.

Faces, voices, books we loved.
There were violets in Chinese bowls.
And, ah, the dancers—

they would hunt us down tonight,
they would caper on our graves.
We lived here—when?—under a spell.
We have awakened. We are here.

"LEAR IS GAY"

(in memory of Betsy)

That gaiety oh
that gaiety I love
has white hair
or thinning or none,

has limbs askew
often as not,
has dimming sight.
Can manage, can

in fevers, rags,
decreptitude.
And oh can laugh
sometimes

at time as at
a scarecrow whose
hobo shoulders are
a-twitch with crows.

A PLAGUE OF STARLINGS

(Fisk Campus)

Evenings I hear
the workmen fire
into the stiff
magnolia leaves,
routing the starlings
gathered noisy and
befouling there.

Their scissoring
terror like glass
coins spilling breaking
the birds explode
into mica sky
raggedly fall
to ground rigid
in clench of cold.

The spared return,
when the guns are through,
to the spoiled trees
like choiceless poor
to a dangerous
dwelling place,
chitter and quarrel
in the piercing dark
above the killed.

Mornings, I pick
my way past death's
black droppings:
on campus lawns
and streets
the troublesome
starlings
frost-salted lie,
troublesome still.

And if not careful
I shall tread
upon carcasses
carcasses when I
go mornings now
to lecture on
what Socrates,
the hemlock hour nigh,
told sorrowing
Phaedo and the rest
about the migratory
habits of the soul.